HANDS-ON AB

ABC Mini Books

by Marilynn G. Barr

LAB20144P
Hands-on ABCs
ABC MINI BOOKS
by Marilynn G. Barr

Published by: Little Acorn Books™
Originally published by: Monday Morning Books, Inc.

Little Acorn Books
PO Box 8787
Greensboro, NC 27419-0787

Promoting Early Skills for a Lifetime™

Little Acorn Books™
is an imprint of Little Acorn Associates, Inc.

http://www.littleacornbooks.com

ISBN 978-1-937257-65-1

Printed in the United States of America

ABC Mini Books Contents

ABC Mini Books Introduction

ABC Mini Books is one of four Hands-on ABC books (**ABC Scissor Skills, ABC Art,** and **ABC Games**) designed to provide alphabet skills practice for early learners. Children practice recognizing letters and letter sounds, associating letters with alphabet pictures, and letter writing.

Each Mini Book consists of eight pages: a cover and seven alphabet picture pages with matching words for each letter of the alphabet. Also included is a letter tracing Mini Book (pp. 58-64) for children to practice writing letters.

How to Make Mini Books

Reproduce the pages for each Mini Book. Cut apart the pages along the dotted lines. Then stack the cut-out pages in sequence and staple to form a Mini Book.

Classroom Mini Books

Reproduce a complete set of Mini Books for use in the classroom. Color, laminate, and cut apart the pages. Stack each set of pages in sequence, then staple to form individual books. Place the Mini Books in a decorated shoe box for children to read individually or with a partner.

Take-home Mini Books

Mini Books make great take-home skills practice activities to share with family members and friends. Reproduce and provide each child with a set of Mini Book pages and the assembly directions on page 5.

My Alphabet Tracing Mini Book

Reproduce a set of alphabet tracing Mini Book pages (pp. 58-64) for each child. Help each child cut apart, stack, and staple their pages together to form tracing Mini Books. Provide crayons or markers for children to decorate the front page of their books. Help each child write his or her name on page 2 of the book. Children can take these books home to practice tracing.

Poster-sized Books

Individual Letter Books: Enlarge each set of Mini Book pages to fit on letter-size sheets of oak tag. You will need eight sheets of oak tag for each book. Cut apart and glue each page onto a separate sheet of oak tag, then laminate. Provide wipe-off crayons or markers for children to color the pictures while they read the books.

Alphabet Tracing Books: Enlarge the alphabet tracing pages (pp. 58-64) to fit on letter-size sheets of oak tag. You will need seven sheets of oak tag. Cut apart and glue each page onto a separate sheet of oak tag, then laminate. Provide wipe-off crayons or markers for children to practice tracing the letters. Decorate a cardboard box to store the books and wipe-off crayons or markers.

 LAB20144P • ABC MINI BOOKS • 978-1-937257-65-1 • © 2014 Little Acorn Books™

How to Assemble

a Mini Book

1. Cut apart the pages on the dotted lines.

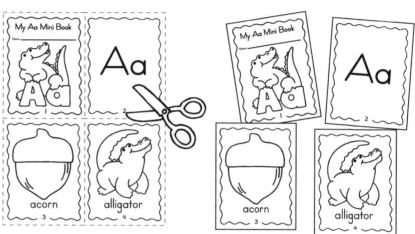

2. Color each page.

3. Stack the pages in the correct order.

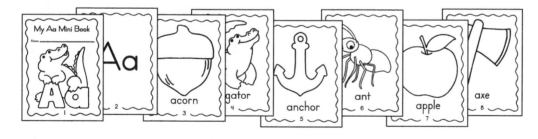

4. Staple the pages to form a book.

My Aa Mini Book

Name _____

1

Aa

2

acorn

3

alligator

4

LAB20144P • ABC MINI BOOKS • 978-1-937257-65-1 • © 2014 Little Acorn Books™

anchor

5

ant

6

apple

7

axe

8

My Bb Mini Book

Name _____

1

B b

2

balloon

3

barn

4

LAB20144P • ABC MINI BOOKS • 978-1-937257-65-1 • © 2014 Little Acorn Books

bell

5

bird

6

bow

7

bus

8

My Cc Mini Book

Name _____

1

Cc

2

cake

3

cat

4

LAB20144P • ABC MINI BOOKS • 978-1-937257-65-1 • © 2014 Little Acorn Books™

caterpillar

5

cow

6

crayon

7

crown

8

My Dd Mini Book

Name _____

1

Dd

2

dinosaur

3

dog

4

 LAB20144P • ABC MINI BOOKS • 978-1-937257-65-1 • © 2014 Little Acorn Books

doll

5

dolphin

6

drum

7

duck

8

My Ee Mini Book

Name _____

1

E e

2

easel

3

egg

4

LAB20144P • ABC MINI BOOKS • 978-1-937257-65-1 • © 2014 Little Acorn Books™

elephant

5

elf

6

envelope

7

eye

8

My Ff Mini Book

Name _____

F f

1

2

feather

3

fish

4

LAB20144P • ABC MINI BOOKS • 978-1-937257-65-1 • © 2014 Little Acorn Books™

flag

5

flower

6

fork

7

frog

8

My Gg Mini Book

Name _____

Gg

1

Gg

2

ghost

3

glasses

4

LAB20144P • ABC MINI BOOKS • 978-1-937257-65-1 • © 2014 Little Acorn Books

glove

5

goose

6

grapes

7

guitar

8

My Hh Mini Book

Name _____

1

H h

2

hammer

3

hat

4

LAB20144P • ABC MINI BOOKS • 978-1-937257-65-1 • © 2014 Little Acorn Books™

heart

5

hippopotamus

6

horse

7

house

8

My Ii Mini Book

Name _____

I i

2

ice cream

3

ice

4

LAB20144P • ABC MINI BOOKS • 978-1-937257-65-1 • © 2014 Little Acorn Books™

ice skate

5

igloo

6

ink

7

iron

8

My Jj Mini Book

Name _____

Jj

2

jack

3

jack-in-the-box

4

 LAB20144P • ABC MINI BOOKS • 978-1-937257-65-1 • © 2014 Little Acorn Books

jack-o'-lantern

5

jar

6

jeep

7

jump rope

8

My Kk Mini Book

Name _____

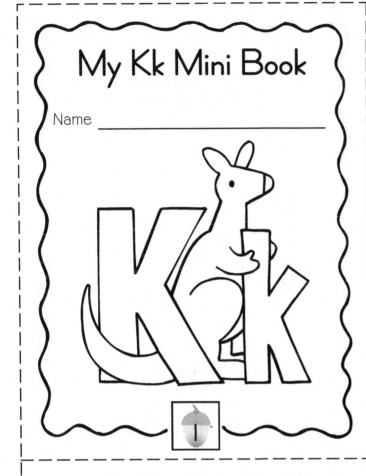

1

K k

2

kangaroo

3

kettle

4

LAB20144P • ABC MINI BOOKS • 978-1-937257-65-1 • © 2014 Little Acorn Books™

key

5

king

6

kite

7

koala

8

My Ll Mini Book

Name _____

2

ladybug

3

lamb

4

LAB20144P • ABC MINI BOOKS • 978-1-937257-65-1 • © 2014 Little Acorn Books™

leaf

5

lion

6

lizard

7

lock

8

My Mm Mini Book

Name _____

Mm

Mm

2

mask

3

mitten

4

LAB20144P • ABC MINI BOOKS • 978-1-937257-65-1 • © 2014 Little Acorn Books

monkey

5

moon

6

moose

7

mouse

8

My Nn Mini Book

Name _____

1

Nn

2

narwhal

3

necklace

4

LAB20144P • ABC MINI BOOKS • 978-1-937257-65-1 • © 2014 Little Acorn Books

needle

5

nest

6

net

7

nine

8

My Oo Mini Book

Name _____

1

O o

2

octopus

3

orangutan

4

LAB20144P • ABC MINI BOOKS • 978-1-937257-65-1 • © 2014 Little Acorn Books

ornament

5

ostrich

6

overalls

7

owl

8

My Pp Mini Book

Name _____

P p

1

2

pail

3

pencil

4

LAB20144P • ABC MINI BOOKS • 978-1-937257-65-1 • © 2014 Little Acorn Books

pie

5

pig

6

pot

7

pumpkin

8

My Qq Mini Book

Name _____

1

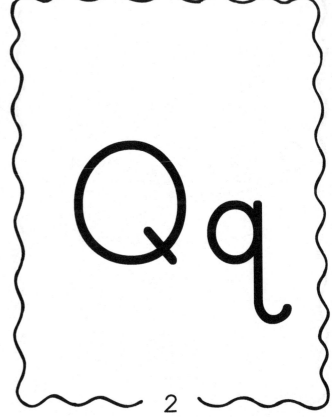

2

quail

3

quarter

4

 LAB20144P • ABC MINI BOOKS • 978-1-937257-65-1 • © 2014 Little Acorn Books™

queen

5

question mark

6

quiet

7

quilt

8

My Rr Mini Book

Name _____

1

R r

2

rabbit

3

raccoon

4

 LAB20144P • ABC MINI BOOKS • 978-1-937257-65-1 • © 2014 Little Acorn Books™

reindeer

5

rhinoceros

6

roller skate

7

rooster

8

My Ss Mini Book

Name _____

S s

2

scissors

3

shell

4

LAB20144P • ABC MINI BOOKS • 978-1-937257-65-1 • © 2014 Little Acorn Books

shoe

5

skunk

6

snake

7

sock

8

My Tt Mini Book

Name _____

Tt

1

T t

2

tambourine

3

telephone

4

LAB20144P • ABC MINI BOOKS • 978-1-937257-65-1 • © 2014 Little Acorn Books

tiger

5

tricycle

6

turkey

7

turtle

8

Name _____

Uu

1

Uu

2

umbrella

3

umpire

4

 LAB20144P • ABC MINI BOOKS • 978-1-937257-65-1 • © 2014 Little Acorn Books™

unicorn

5

unicycle

6

underwear

7

United States

8

My Vv Mini Book

Name _____

Vv

vacuum
3

van
4

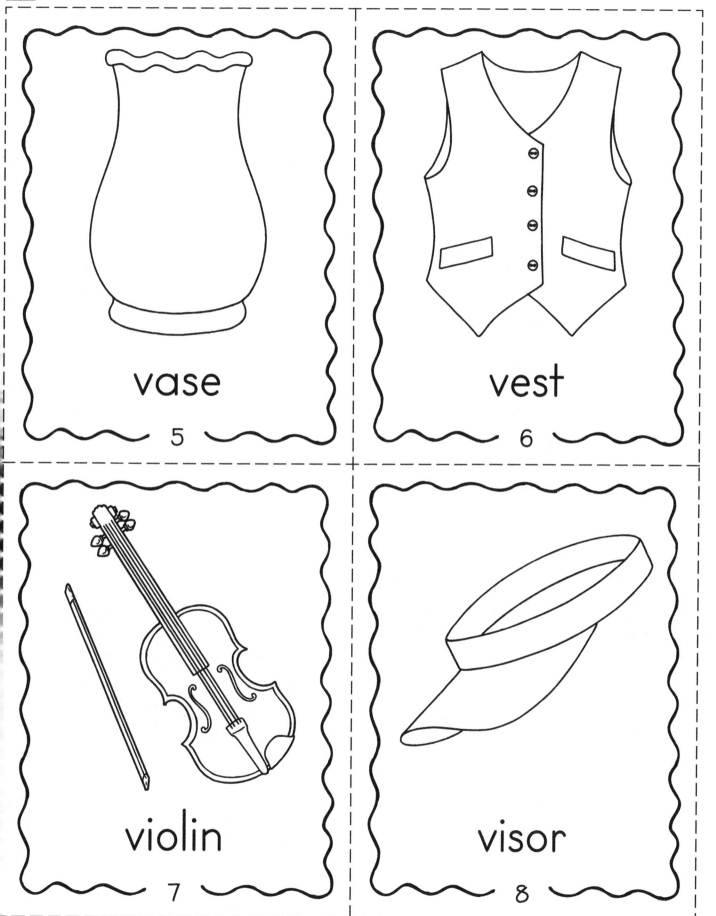

vase

5

vest

6

violin

7

visor

8

My Ww Mini Book

Name _____

W

W

1

Ww

2

walrus

3

watermelon

4

 LAB20144P • ABC MINI BOOKS • 978-1-937257-65-1 • © 2014 Little Acorn Books™

web

5

whale

6

whistle

7

wig

8

My Xx Mini Book

Name _____

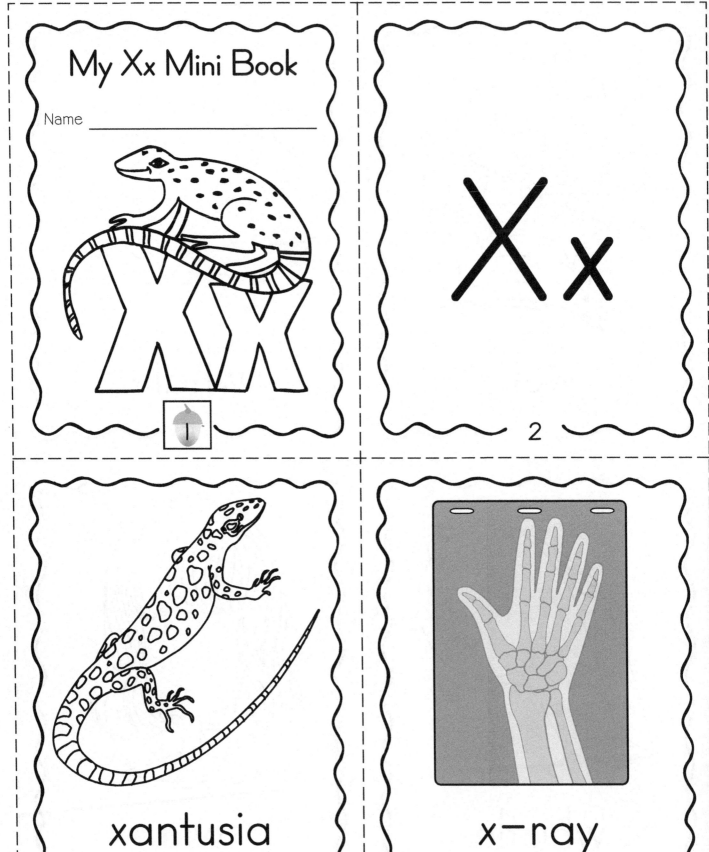

X x

2

xantusia

3

x-ray

4

LAB20144P • ABC MINI BOOKS • 978-1-937257-65-1 • © 2014 Little Acorn Books™

xylophone

5

My Yy Mini Book

Name _____

Y y

2

yak

3

yarn

4

 LAB20144P • ABC MINI BOOKS • 978-1-937257-65-1 • © 2014 Little Acorn Books

yawn

5

yellow

6

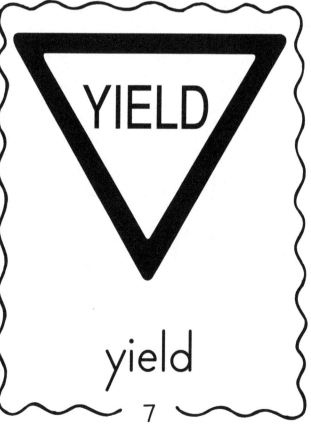

yield

7

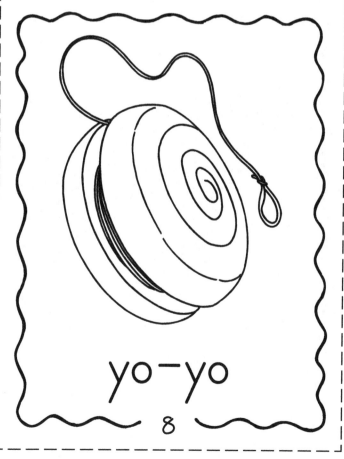

yo-yo

8

My Zz Mini Book

Name _____

1

Z z

2

zebra

3

zebu

4

 LAB20144P • ABC MINI BOOKS • 978-1-937257-65-1 • © 2014 Little Acorn Books™

zero

5

zigzag

6

zipper

7

zither

8

My Alphabet Tracing Mini Book

This book belongs to

_____

Name

1

2

LAB20144P • ABC MINI BOOKS • 978-1-937257-65-1 • © 2014 Little Acorn Books™

LAB20144P • ABC MINI BOOKS • 978-1-937257-65-1 • © 2014 Little Acorn Books

LAB20144P • ABC MINI BOOKS • 978-1-937257-65-1 • © 2014 Little Acorn Books™

S
s
19

T
t
20

U
u
21

V
v
22

LAB20144P • ABC MINI BOOKS • 978-1-937257-65-1 • © 2014 Little Acorn Books™

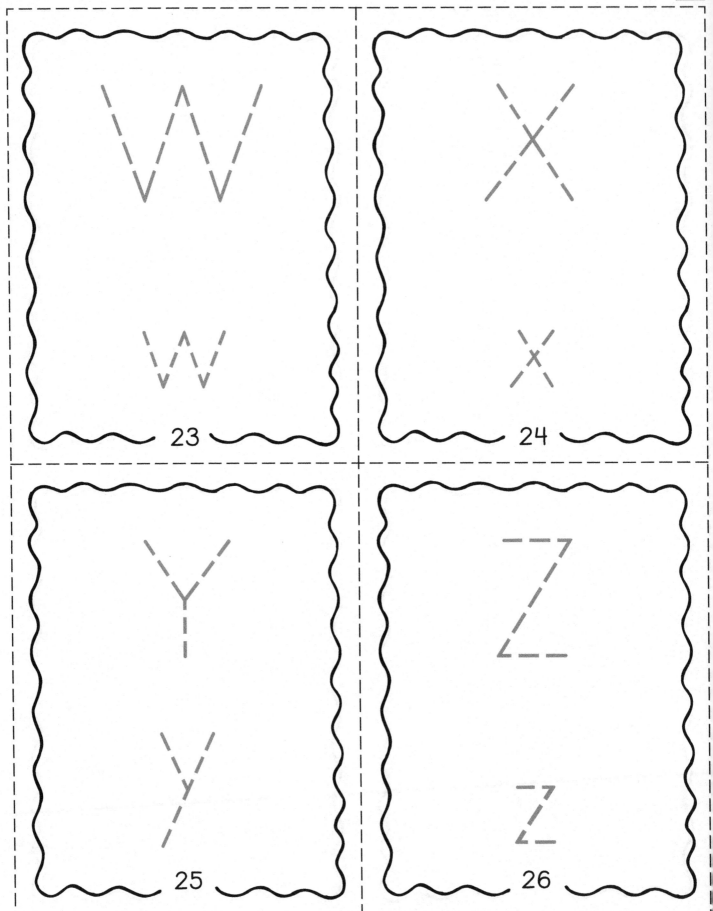

LAB20144P • ABC MINI BOOKS • 978-1-937257-65-1 • © 2014 Little Acorn Books™

Little Acorn Books™

Promoting Early Skills for a Lifetime™

A Hands-on Picture Book Series Designed to Foster Early Skills • Infancy–Age 4

Best Seller

Using Crayons,
Scissors, & Glue
for Crafts
Preschool–Grade 1

Miss Pitty Pat
& Friends
Preschool–Grade 1

Mookie's
Christmas Tree
Not Just for Christmas

Hands-On ABCs • ABC and Readiness Skills Practice for Early Learners

Made in the USA
Middletown, DE
09 December 2018